RAILWAY HISTORY IN PICTURES: THE MIDLANDS

This painting by Victor Welch depicts two Midland Railway Kirtley goods engines on a freight train near Wigston about 1920. A typical Midlands scene of the period.

RAILWAY HISTORY IN PICTURES

The Midlands

H. C. CASSERLEY
C. C. DORMAN

DAVID & CHARLES : NEWTON ABBOT

7153 4687 3

Printed in Great Britain by
E. Goodman & Son Limited Taunton
for David & Charles (Publishers) Limited
South Devon House Newton Abbot Devon

CONTENTS

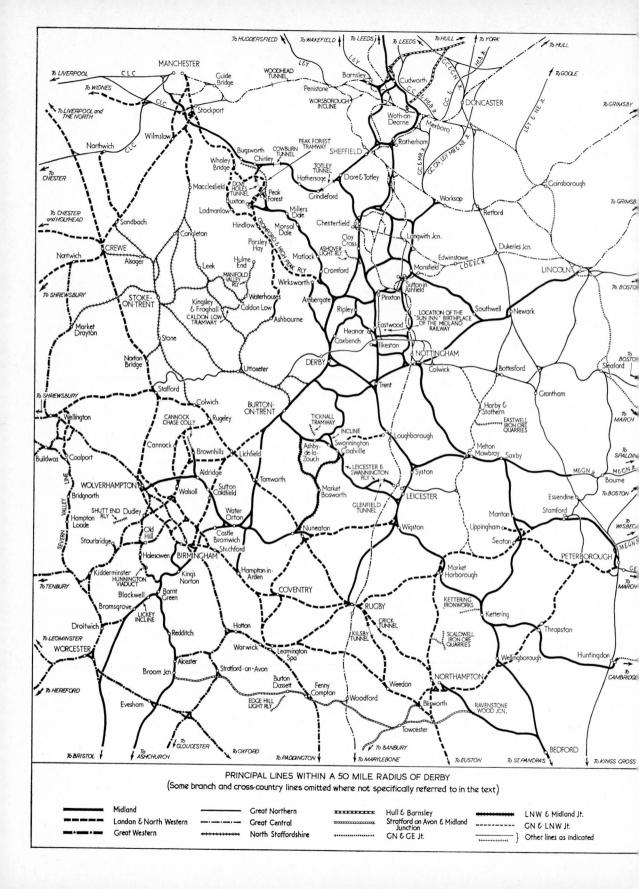

PRINCIPAL LINES WITHIN A 50 MILE RADIUS OF DERBY

(Some branch and cross-country lines omitted where not specifically referred to in the text)

Midland	Great Northern	Hull & Barnsley	LNW & Midland Jt.
London & North Western	Great Central	Stratford on Avon & Midland Junction	GN & LNW Jt.
Great Western	North Staffordshire	GN & GE Jt.	} Other lines as indicated

INTRODUCTION

The Midlands has always been a difficult area to define; for instance, in the days when Northamptonshire cricket was at a low ebb, one of our most respectable London newspapers wrote of 'that Midland side which has so often helped prop up the County Championship table'. It was a different matter when they began to challenge the leaders; then they joined those other 'southern' contenders, ie, Surrey and Middlesex! Perhaps this example may help to make clear one of the initial difficulties which in the end we resolved by taking as our yard-stick an arbitrary radius from Derby, which in railway circles may well be considered the centre of the Midlands.

We decided on a distance of fifty miles, which we found allowed us to include some photographs of two such widely diverse subjects as Crewe Works and the standard and narrow-gauge lines serving the Northamptonshire iron ore fields. Our troubles were by no means over when this decision had been taken, for we were then faced with the mass of items of railway interest which have their origins in the Midlands. Suffice it to say that some items, such as the London & Birmingham, the 'Knotty', and the Lickey Incline, chose themselves, but generally speaking much must have inevitably been omitted, and conversely some items included which could well have been left out. However, this book is primarily intended as a pictorial vignette and as such can only supply the merest glimpse of the Midlands railway scene. Consequently we can only hope that this glimpse may arouse sufficient interest to awaken the desire to know more about some of the fascinating subjects which were once, and in many cases still are, a vital part of the thrusting and important industrial area which Belloc so unfairly described as 'sodden and unkind'.

There can be few more beautiful railway journeys than those once available through the wooded Shropshire countryside, journeys alas no longer possible owing to the closures; the Leek & Manifold had a charm of its own which may well have been equalled by some other light railways, but surely never surpassed. Of the main lines which traverse the area, the old North Western between Rugby and Crewe carried the most traffic, much of it being through services, but for all that, it provided some inspiring sights for the railway enthusiast; for example, the approach of an express to the north, rounding Queensville Curve just south of Stafford station. The Great Western impressed its own imperishable style wherever it was to be found, be it the Bewdley to Bridgnorth local nosing gently behind a Dean 0-6-0 beside the bank of the Severn, adjacent to the Wye Forest, or the 2.10 Paddington to Birkenhead roaring through Banbury with a 'Castle' at its head.

The impeccable trains of the Midland Railway crossed the area from south-west to east, with many a thriving branch, and shared New Street Station, Birmingham (one of the largest and busiest in the United Kingdom) with the North Western. Birmingham's other main line station, Snow Hill, was one of the lightest and cleanest of all big city stations, but is unfortunately likely to be closed to passenger traffic in the near future, consequent upon the enlargement of the redeveloped New Street, and the electrification of the old London & North Western lines using that station. Many of the old Great Western services will use the latter station; others will terminate at Moor Street.

Further north the busy coal and steel areas of Sheffield and Rotherham provide much to please the railway enthusiast, one of the main attractions being the Wentworth Incline which ranks with the Lickey Incline on the Midland, and the Dainton and Rattery on the GWR as one of the steepest main line banks in the country.

The North Staffordshire Railway was a small prosperous company in the Potteries, quite autonomous in spite of a continuing North Western desire to engulf it; it had a busy commuter service based on Stoke-on-Trent. Further east and south the Great Central Railway, with its handsome locomotives, crossed the Midlands from Nottingham to Aylesbury, via Rugby, and has the unhappy distinction of being the first main line to be closed.

Of the country's narrow-gauge passenger lines, the only ones to fall within the compass of this book were the Leek & Manifold and the Ashover Light Railway, although until recent years there were still some interesting narrow-gauge freight workings such as the ironstone lines in Northamptonshire which were built by the giant steel firms to transport their iron ore to the various steelworks.

Historically, the London & Birmingham is perhaps the focal point but it may be recalled that the Great Western broad-gauge penetrated to Wolverhampton and that the Midland Railway owed its beginnings to amalgamations involving the North Midland, the Birmingham & Derby and the Midland Counties. Architecturally, the Midland area has plenty of all that is best—and worst—in railway practice, and some examples may be found in the ensuing pages.

C. C. DORMAN.

H. C. CASSERLEY

One of Mr Johnson's lovely single-wheelers piloting No 543 on the Lickey Incline (see p 18).

EARLY DAYS

The early railway builders were men of astonishing imagination and will-power. For instance, during the construction of the London to Birmingham Railway, Robert Stephenson walked the entire length of the line twenty times, and it is not surprising that, except for Camden Bank, no gradient on the original line exceeds 1 in 330; to this day there are very few speed restrictions for curves and even in these cases a top speed of 75 mph is usually permitted.

The opening of the Birmingham terminus at Curzon Street on 9 April 1838 was one of the milestones of railway history in the Midlands. At this time there were over 3,000 regular stage-coach routes in the United Kingdom, but by the mid-1850s most of the modern main lines had been constructed and in the middle of this decade there began the period known as the 'Railway Mania', during which some people made vast fortunes, whilst many others lost large sums of money, due to the craze for speculation in railways.

The Midlands, with its many industries, was soon covered by a network of lines, and with the amalgamation in 1846 of the Grand Junction (which had already absorbed the Liverpool & Manchester in 1845), the London & Birmingham, and the Manchester & Birmingham, the four greatest cities in England were connected by the same company ie, the London & North Western Railway.

The Midland Railway was incorporated in 1844 by the amalgamation of the North Midland, the Midland Counties, and the Birmingham & Derby Junction, all of which met at Derby. Derby therefore, became the headquarters of the new concern, and the central focus of what eventually became the wide network not only of the Midland Railway itself but one of the most important centres of the whole British Railway system.

The oldest part of the Midland Railway was the Leicester & Swannington, opened in 1833. It started as an independent concern and was the direct cause of the promotion of the Midland Counties Railway, the oldest of the three original constituents of the Midland. This was the reply of the Derbyshire coal owners to the construction of the Leicester & Swannington as it was feared that the new railway would affect their trade. The Leicester & Swannington was promoted in 1829 and received parliamentary assent on 29 May 1830. The first part was opened on 17 July 1832, with completion in 1833, in which year passenger services commenced. The engineer was the younger Robert Stephenson, son of George Stephenson. The line held the distinction of being not only the first steam operated railway in the Midlands, but one of the earliest in the country. It was absorbed by the Midland Railway in 1846.

From a purely geographical point of view Birmingham can probably lay claim to being the centre of England; but in considering the general aspect of the Midlands, that is, the area of the coal and steel industries and what is known as the Black Country, Derby became a far more logical centre. Not that all of the country within a fifty mile radius is of an industrial nature; it is an area of enormous contrasts, ranging from the coalfields and the drabness of such cities as Stoke-on-Trent, to the beautiful country-side of North Derbyshire through which runs, or did until recently, one of the most picturesque main lines in England to which reference will be made later.

In the early days of railways a strong case was made in favour of a broader gauge than the standard 4 ft 8½ in generally in use, and the Great Western Railway was built to a 7 ft 0¼ in gauge. As it grew and made connections with other companies, a strenuous battle developed as to the professed superiority of the broad gauge. In many places a third rail was laid to allow 4 ft 8½ in gauge vehicles to use the existing lines but in 1848 Parliament decided that there were to be no more broad-gauge lines laid and so the narrower gauge became standard. The GWR realised as early as 1861 that it had to conform to the general standard but it was not until 1892 (22 May) that the final conversion took place.

The earliest penetration of the Great Western into the Midlands (or perhaps in their case more accurately the west Midlands) was in 1852 when the GWR reached Birmingham by way of Banbury, and the Oxford, Worcester & Wolverhampton got as far as Stourbridge. The mixed-gauge line from Banbury was originally incorporated as the Birmingham & Oxford Railway but before its opening, became part of the GWR which had been responsible for its construction. The Oxford, Worcester & Wolverhampton Railway was of standard gauge, and when both lines reached Wolverhampton in 1854, joining at Priestfield Junction, two miles short of Wolverhampton, it was still by way of mixed gauge over the Great Western Railway route. The Oxford, Worcester & Wolverhampton Railway was merged into a new company, the West Midland, in 1860, by amalgamation with the Worcester & Hereford and the Newport, Abergavenny & Hereford, but the new company was short lived and in 1863 became part of the Great Western Railway.

Of the three remaining railways which came into the area of the Midlands, the North Stafford was unique in that the whole of the compact system lies within the prescribed boundaries, and in these circumstances the very brief history of the line, which had its origins in 1846, can best be considered in the subsequent chapter relating specifically to this railway.

The Great Northern, which does not play such an important part in the picture of the Midlands as do the four railways already referred to, may be said to have made its first incursion into the area via the east coast route to Scotland, completed in 1852. In due course the Great Northern Railway reached the Nottinghamshire coalfields and competed with the Midland Railway for the coal traffic in the area, whilst in 1878 it extended westward to Derby and shortly afterwards absorbed the Stafford & Uttoxeter, which had been opened in 1868, thus giving the Great Northern Railway an outlying penetration into the L&NWR preserve of the west Midlands.

The sixth line, the Great Central, was of course the last comer by virtue of its extension to London, powers for which were obtained in 1892. It was destined to be the last main line to be built in this country and also to attain the regrettable distinction of being the first to be closed. Further reference will be found in later chapters.

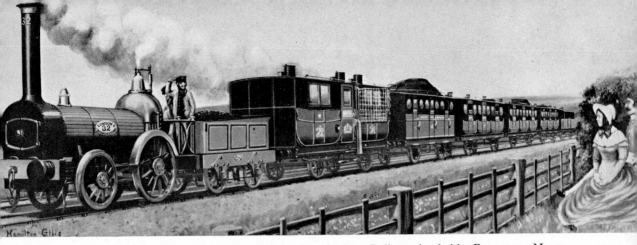

Express mail train on the London & Birmingham Railway, hauled by Bury 2-2-0 No 32.

The Stephensons—father and son.

George Stephenson carried out the surveys, and was principal engineer in the late 1830s for the North Midland and for the Birmingham & Derby railways. He also founded the Clay Cross Collieries in 1837, the first company to send coal to London by rail. He spent the declining years of his life at Tapton House, Chesterfield, where he died on 12 August 1848 at the age of 67 and was buried in Trinity Church, Chesterfield.

Robert Stephenson was appointed chief engineer to the Leicester & Swannington Railway in 1829 at the early age of 25, and shortly afterwards became chief engineer to the London & Birmingham Railway. He died at the age of 56.

The original terminus of the L&BR at Curzon Street, Birmingham.

The construction of Kilsby tunnel, south of Rugby, gave much trouble owing to flooding, but Robert Stephenson was eventually able to cope with the situation by installing this elaborate pumping system, capable of maintaining a flow of 1,800 gallons a minute.

The incline, Leicester & Swannington Railway.

Leicester & Swannington Railway, **Samson,** reputedly the first locomotive to be fitted with a whistle, then known as a steam trumpet.

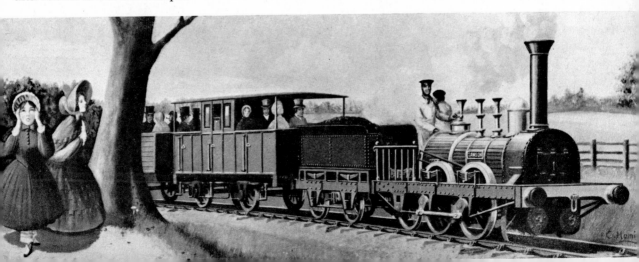

The Leicester & Swannington Railway. The original terminus at West Bridge station, Leicester.

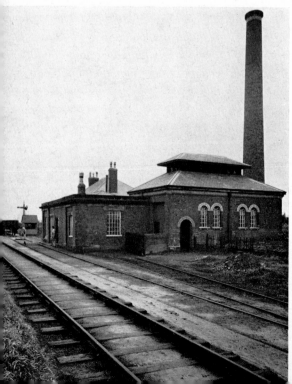

The winding house, Leicester & Swannington Railway. Part of the winding engine, built in 1833, is preserved in the railway museum at York.

14

The inn sign at the Sun, Eastwood, with the original ironwork depicting a Bury 2-2-0. This ancient hostelry is traditionally regarded as the birthplace of the Midland Railway. A meeting was held there on 16 August 1832, the outcome of which was the formation of the Midland Counties Railway, the oldest constituent of the original MR.

Milford Tunnel, near Duffield, North Midland Railway, under construction.

Chesterfield Station, about 1860.

15

An accident on the LNWR at Elwells Park, Bescot, in 1859. The locomotives are thought to be the Southern Division Sharp 0-6-0s of 1848.

16   Reproduction of an early poster of 1843 of the Birmingham & Derby Junction Railway.

THE MIDLAND RAILWAY

The aptly-named Midland Railway, with its far reaching ramifications covering the whole country from London, Bristol, Lancashire, Leeds and Carlisle, and over jointly owned lines to Broadstone in the South and Yarmouth on the east coast, must rank as the most important pre-grouping line serving the centre of England. As recorded in Chapter 1, it was incorporated in 1844 by the amalgamation of three railways, all converging on Derby. One of these was the Midland Counties, the first section of which was opened from Derby to Nottingham in 1839 as a rival line to the Leicester & Swannington Railway. This latter had been opened in 1832 and was one of the earliest steam operated lines in the country. The Leicester & Swannington was absorbed by the MR in 1846 and as a result became the oldest part of that company's system. It survived, for freight traffic only, until quite recently.

So far as the locomotives of the MR are concerned, one may recall briefly that during the period 1844-1923 there were only four locomotive superintendents or chief mechanical engineers: Matthew Kirtley was in office until 1873 when he was succeeded by Mr S. W. Johnson whose reign lasted until 1903. During this time Johnson built a large number of very efficient locomotives, noted particularly for their neat outlines and good looks, some of which were considered by many to be amongst the most handsome ever designed. He also introduced that wonderful colour, Midland lake, which was used for both engines and carriages. In a slightly modified form the colour persisted through LMS days and has only recently disappeared, giving way to the new, all pervading BR blue.

Johnson's last engines were his most famous three-cylinder compounds, five of which came out in 1902-3. They were later modified by his successor, Mr R. M. Deeley, who built another forty, and the class was perpetuated by Sir Henry Fowler, after the grouping, to an ultimate total of 240 engines, all of which lasted into BR days.

Pictures of a representative selection of Midland engines follow these pages, but further MR illustrations will be found accompanying several other chapters.

The Midland was certainly a splendid railway from many points of view, particularly in its cleanliness and the neat and tidy appearance not only of its trains but also of the stations and permanent way. Its convenient services, coupled with a high standard of comfort and punctuality, made it exceedingly popular with the regular traveller. Much of the rise and progress to prosperity of the Midland was due in no small measure to the vigorous policies of James Allport, general manager from 1853 to 1880, and afterwards a director. He received a well deserved knighthood in 1884 and died at the Midland Grand Hotel at St Pancras in 1892, one of the greater figures of British railway history outside the ranks of the famous engineers.

Sir James Allport who did so much to further the cause of the Midland Railway, and S. W. Johnson, chief mechanical engineer from 1873 to 1903 who designed some of the most beautiful engines ever built.

Early view of a Kirtley 2-4-0 built in 1864 and broken up in 1887.

Mr Johnson's standard passenger tank class in the immaculate condition in which the engines were kept under his superintendency.

Kirtley 2-4-0 No 901 on a Pullman car train in 1880.

Johnson class 2 0-6-0 No 1365, a class of which several hundred were built, with a mixed train comprising three Pullman cars.

The Midland introduced the American Pullman car to this country in 1874 at the instigation of Sir James Allport. They provided a standard of comfort and excellence hitherto unknown in this country.

A Midland bogie family saloon of 1879.

THE LONDON & NORTH WESTERN

Self-styled as Britain's 'Premier Line', a title open to some argument as supporters of the rival GWR and Midland lines are quick to point out, the LNWR embraces the main line dividing at Rugby for Birmingham (the original London & Birmingham Railway); the Grand Junction, which continued northwards to Crewe, Liverpool and Manchester; and the Trent Valley line through Lichfield to Stafford. Crewe, that most famous railway junction of all time, was the centre and hub of the old LNWR in the same way that Derby was of the Midland.

The LNWR built practically all of its locomotives at Crewe; in the early days under Alexander Allan, followed by John Ramsbottom, who was succeeded in turn by F. W. Webb, who reigned from 1871 until 1903. He was followed by George Whale, Bowen-Cooke, Beames, and finally George Hughes of the L&YR, with which railway the LNWR amalgamated in 1922, a year prior to the grouping.

F. W. Webb has suffered the misfortune of being remembered by his failures, his three-cylinder 'double single wheeled' compounds, with which he obstinately persevered even after it had become abundantly clear that they were, at best, extremely unreliable, and more often than not a headache to the operating department. In his favour one should not lose sight of the fact that he built large numbers of very efficient locomotives of simple but sturdy construction; his various classes of 2-4-0s in particular, and his numerous 0-6-0s, 0-6-2Ts and other types, all gave very many years of useful service.

When he succeeded Webb in 1903, Whale very soon cleared out the worst of the compounds and introduced very different designs of his own, The 'Precursors' in particular revolutionised the working of the crack trains, and Bowen-Cooke, who succeeded Whale in 1909 developed them into the remarkable 'George the Fifths'. Later Bowen-Cooke also produced the LNWR's largest express passenger engines, the four-cylinder 4-6-0 'Claughtons', whose ultimate history did not altogether fulfil their excellent promise, but which nevertheless did a lot of good work up to the time of the grouping.

The North Western was an aristocratic line and had in former days many outstanding personalities at its head, amongst which stand out the autocratic engineer F. W. Webb already referred to; the redoubtable chairman, Sir Richard Moon; and before him, that astute business man, Sir Mark Huish, who had come from the Grand Junction and for a time became the virtual dictator of the LNWR. Harsh and inexorable these men may have been, but it is doubtful whether without them the North Western would have risen to the heights it eventually attained.

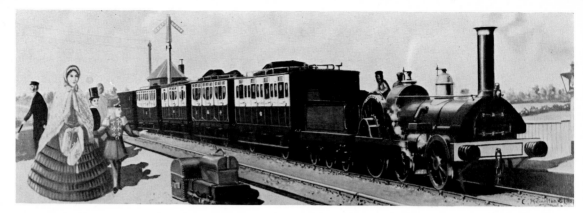

An early LNWR scene: Crampton locomotive **Courier** at Sandbach about 1850.

LNWR scene of 1865.

LNWR scene of 1875.

'Ramsbottom DX goods' No 3315 as rebuilt, at Birmingham New Street.

Ramsbottom 2-2-2 'Lady of the Lake' class No 127 **Peel.** Sixty were built between 1859 and 1865, some of which lasted into the early years of the present century.

Webb 2-2-2-2 Compound **Richard Trevithick.**

Old LNWR four-wheeled coach on the Manchester-Buxton branch.

A fine twelve-wheeled dining car of 1905 built for the through service between London and Scotland in conjunction with the Caledonian Railway.

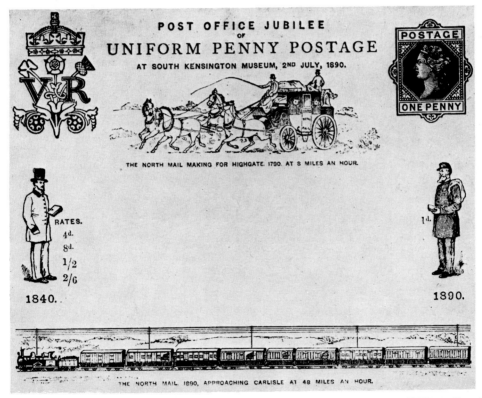

Reproduction of a special cover issued by the Post Office in 1890, depicting a LNWR mail train of the period. This is the nearest to a railway stamp ever produced in this country, despite the fact that Britain was the pioneer of railways which were directly responsible for the industrial revolution. The omission is all the more inexplicable in view of the present floods of commemorative stamps, often showing subjects of comparatively minor importance.

THE NORTH STAFFORD

Of all the six principal pre-grouping railways which are encompassed by the area within a radius of fifty miles of Derby, the North Stafford is unique in that the whole of its system comes inside the arbitrary boundary.

The North Stafford, or 'Knotty' as it was nicknamed because of its distinctive emblem in the form of a knot, was a busy and compact railway, and although not comparable in size with the giants, by no means a minor one. It might perhaps be described either as one of the largest and most important of the lesser railways, or one of the smallest of the major ones.

The North Stafford Railway was incorporated in 1845 and the first section open for traffic ran between Stoke and Norton Bridge on the Grand Junction line. By 1849 the company controlled 112 miles of route and connected with the London & North Western Railway and the Midland Railway. To avoid a threatened junction with the Great Western at Wednesbury, the North Western proposed amalgamation on terms most profitable to the North Stafford, but Parliament refused this under the Railway and Canal Traffic Act. Consequently the North Stafford retained its sovereignty until sixty years later. Their distinctive red trains and smart little engines were to be seen in Manchester, Derby, Nottingham, Birmingham and Rugby. It even operated, jointly with the North Western, a through express from Manchester to Euston via Stoke, and at one period, on summer Saturdays, a North Stafford Railway loco worked through to Llandudno. Literally at the other end of the scale it operated the Leek & Manifold 2 ft 3 in gauge light railway whose engines and coaches were all painted in North Stafford crimson.

The centre and hub of the NSR was the Potteries town of Stoke-on-Trent, or rather the 'five towns' as the area is usually known, consisting of Stoke, Hanley, Burslem, Fenton and Tunstall. A quarter of a million people live in a space of nine miles by three, one of the most densely populated areas of the British Isles.

To work the busy system, the NSR in its last years had a fleet of some two hundred locomotives, of which over half were 0-6-0 tender and tank engines. There were forty 0-6-2Ts, mostly employed on the busy passenger services radiating from Stoke (now reduced to a mere shadow, with many lines closed entirely). These were supplemented by some 0-6-4Ts, 2-4-2Ts, 0-4-4Ts and 2-4-0Ts. What may be considered the 'main line' engines for working through to Manchester and between Derby and Crewe, were five 4-4-0s and seven 4-4-2Ts.

The whole of the NSR loco stock fared badly under the grouping for the LMS were very quick to replace them with their own types, mainly of MR and LNWR origin. Later new designs, particularly Fowler 2-6-4Ts, were introduced so that as early as 1939 the last NSR engine had been withdrawn from service. However, a number had been sold to collieries and other industrial concerns and fortunately one of these, an 0-6-2T No 2, has survived to be preserved.

Why the North Stafford was nicknamed 'The Knotty'. This distinctive emblem was to be found in all sorts of places, including the stove in the waiting room at Stone station.

Early view of a train near Stoke; the artist's impression gives a good idea of the Potteries district.

An old picture of a local NSR train, the Knot emblem can again be seen distinctly on the engine and coaches.

Leek station, NSR, about fifty years ago.

In pre-grouping days, double-headed trains, hauled by locomotives of more than one company, were virtually unknown, but such a scene could be witnessed on occasions on the NSR, as seen in this photograph of a LNWR DX goods piloting a NSR 2-4-0.

4-4-2T No 8 at Stone in 1915. A LNWR train can be seen in the background.

Stoke shed about 1935.

THE GREAT WESTERN

The Great Western cannot be regarded as having been a central figure in the Midlands and only came into the picture to any extent by virtue of its main line through Birmingham and Wolverhampton, the heart of the Black Country. The principal activities of that great company lay of course more in the ramifications of its vast network in the West of England and South Wales.

However, its foothold in Warwickshire and Staffordshire, which may be regarded as the fringe of its territory, resulted in its being no mean factor in this area, which may perhaps reasonably be described as the west Midlands. A very brief account of how it reached the Black Country is given in Chapter 1. This main line did of course extend northwards to Shrewsbury and Chester, but that does not come within the boundaries of our present review. Mention should, however, be made of its penetrating line from Wellington northwards through Market Drayton where it made contact with the North Stafford, a somewhat unlikely juxtaposition of two railways entirely different, both in size and nature. The line joined the LNWR at Nantwich and was actually able to run its own trains into Crewe. This, however, was only a secondary cross-country line, little more than an elongated branch, which lost its meagre passenger service in 1963.

So far as Birmingham and Wolverhampton were concerned, the GWR was a very important factor, both being situated on its main line carrying through trains, both day and night, between Paddington and Birkenhead. The GWR also had a busy network of local lines serving such places as Dudley, Stourbridge and Kidderminster, all of which used to enjoy a quite intensive passenger service. The GWR's fine station at Birmingham Snow Hill is now virtually closed; its through expresses from London are no more, all being diverted to, and terminated at, the rival North Western's modernised New Street station, with the local traffic a shadow of its former self.

The importance of Birmingham to the GWR in former days is evidenced by the large locomotive shed at Tyseley, which housed examples of almost all the principal Great Western types, At Wolverhampton it even maintained a large locomotive works, second only in importance to Swindon. All of this is now past history.

The famous 'Kings' took their share in working the principal trains between London and Wolverhampton, a small allocation of them being stationed at Stafford Road shed for these duties.

The Great Western always seems to have had rather more than its fair share of whole-hearted devotees, and succeeded in retaining its peculiar individuality right through the grouping years until nationalisation, and even to some extent thereafter. There was a continuous tradition stemming from its succession of noted engineers—Brunel, the Armstrongs, Dean and Churchward—not to be found on any other railway over such a long period.

Standard-gauge tracks at Wednesbury in 1895. The width between the tracks indicates the space formerly required by the 7 ft gauge.

Dean single-wheeler No 3050 **Royal Sovereign** at Stourbridge Junction.

4-4-0 No 3531 with a local, passing Handsworth Junction.

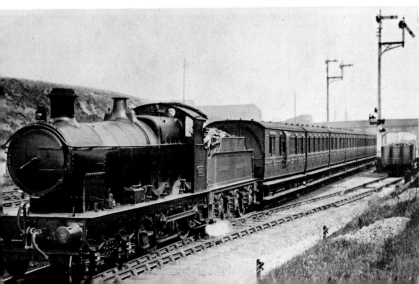

Phlegethon, one of a type of broad-gauge engines which worked in the Birmingham district.

2-6-2T No 3920, rebuilt from a Dean 0-6-0 tender engine, at Stourbridge Junction.

Three developments of rail motors, which the GWR used to a considerable extent on local services and branch lines:

Steam rail-motor at Himley (closed to passengers in 1932).

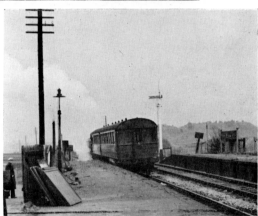

Old Hill to Dudley train leaving Windmill End, September 1956.

Diesel railcar at Dudley, September 1956.

The picturesque station at Kidderminster.

The last steam locomotive to be overhauled at Wolverhampton works, February 1964.

34

THE GREAT NORTHERN

The Great Northern was a comparative late-comer to the Midlands, for the MR, LNWR, and NSR were well established in the centre of the country by the 1840s and the GWR by 1852. The final section of the GNR east coast route, that between Peterborough and Newark, was not completed until 1852. There was already in existence the Nottingham & Grantham Railway (then known under the grandiose title of Ambergate, Nottingham & Boston & Eastern Junction Railway) which joined up with the GNR at Grantham, and by virtue of running powers the Great Northern gained access to Nottingham, but was dependent at first on access over the Midland line under an agreement of 1854. A new station at Nottingham London Road was built in 1857, rendering the GNR independent of the Midland, and the Nottingham & Grantham Railway was leased to the Great Northern in 1861. Through coal traffic had still to be carried over the MR and, because of a dispute over rates, the GNR decided to promote its own lines into the coalfield. A branch from Colwick to Pinxton was opened in 1875, extended westwards to Derby in 1878 and, by virtue of running powers over the North Stafford, GNR trains were able to run to Burton. The absorption of the Stafford & Uttoxeter Railway, opened in 1868, finally gave the Great Northern access to an area hitherto the sole preserve of the LNWR.

The locomotive history falls into four periods: the Sturrock regime from 1850 to 1866, followed by the renowned Patrick Stirling who was in office until 1895 and was succeeded by H. A. Ivatt who in turn was followed in 1911 by the famous Sir Nigel Gresley, who not only covered the remainder of the Great Northern's existence as a separate company, but was also for several years chief mechanical engineer of the LNER.

Stirling is of course best remembered by his famous 8 ft singles, the first of which is preserved in York Museum. Ivatt probably for introducing the 'Atlantic' type to Great Britain, and Sir Nigel Gresley for his well known 'Pacifics' introduced in 1922. The 'Pacifics' were exemplified by the **Flying Scotsman** familiar to all present day enthusiasts and by the later streamlined version, the A4s, of which **Mallard,** with its properly authenticated world record, now rests in York Museum.

Nottingham to Bottesford train near
Radcliffe-on-Trent.

35

Westerly outpost of the GNR; a train running into Stafford with 2-4-0 No 868.

Local train at Tutbury, 1933, with rebuilt Stirling 0-6-0 No 4094.

The GNR Stafford line lost its passenger service in December 1939. It was completely closed in 1957, and this picture shows one of the last trains, a special rail tour, at Chartley and Stowe on 23 March 1957.

Typical stations on the Nottingham-Derby line.

The branch train at Pinxton, September 1955, J6 0-6-0 No 64235.

An old view of Colwick yard.

THE GREAT CENTRAL

The Great Central was the last-comer on the Midland scene, when the old Manchester, Sheffield & Lincolnshire extended itself to London, an ambition which it realised in 1899. Its first expresses were smartly timed and extremely comfortable trains for their period, equal, if not actually superior, to those to be found on the rival Midland line, and with a higher proportion of corridor stock. It was the first railway to develop buffet cars on many cross country trains, as for instance the through service between Newcastle and Swansea. This passed into GCR hands at Sheffield, travelled through the new grandiose station at Nottingham Victoria (built jointly with the GNR), then on to Leicester. It would cross the LNWR main line at Rugby and hand over to the GWR at Banbury.

Services over the GCR London extension were at first worked by the Pollitt 4-2-2s, six in number, and 4-4-0s, but these soon gave way to the 4-4-0s and 'Atlantics' of J. G. Robinson, who was chief mechanical engineer from 1900 until 1922. Robinson is noted as having produced many very handsome designs, his early 4-4-0s and the 'Atlantics' in particular, and also for having been responsible for the ubiquitous 04 2-8-0s, built in large numbers and used overseas in both world wars. One of these engines is now happily assured of a permanent place in Leicester Museum.

The GCR London Extension under construction. View north of Sherwood Rise Tunnel.

Two more views of the GCR London Extension under construction at the end of the nineteenth century. Nottingham cutting route through the city centre and a construction depot near Bulwell.

One of Mr Pollitt's beautiful single-wheelers built for the London Extension.

No 192, one of Mr Robinson's handsome 'Atlantics', at Nottingham Victoria in 1923, shortly after the grouping.

Rebuilt Robinson 4-4-0, LNER No 6016, at Annesley in 1926 on the 'Dido' workman's train, which ran to carry enginemen and staff from this somewhat isolated depot to and from their homes, sometimes three or four miles distant.

Robinson inside-cylinder 4-6-0 No 5424 **City of Lincoln,** at Sheffield in 1926.

Possibly Mr Robinson's most successful design, his 2-8-0, of which several hundred were built, and which saw much service overseas during both world wars. No 6227 is seen here on the Great Northern main line, passing Dukeries Junction in 1947.

Lancashire, Derbyshire & East Coast 0-6-4T No 29 (later GCR No 1148).

Robinson 2-8-0 No 6625 as rebuilt by Mr Thompson, passing Dunford Bridge old station in 1946.

The handsome Great Central war memorial on Mexborough station, in commemoration of local GCR employees who gave their lives during the first world war.

IMPORTANT RAILWAY CENTRES—DERBY

Derby not only forms the focal point of the area covered by this book but, as headquarters of the old Midland Railway, was also a very important railway centre in its own right, having the same relationship to the MR as had Crewe to the North Western or Darlington to the North Eastern. The Great Western had no comparable central pivot, unless possibly Bristol could be so regarded.

The original train shed was built by the North Midland Railway and survived for many years, for although the station was rebuilt at various times, the shed did not disappear until the 1950s. The present-day station bears little resemblance to the former one, although the arrangement of the six platforms remains much the same.

As the main workshop of the Midland system, all types of engines were naturally to be seen in profusion. Many of them were visible from the main line of the station itself, unlike some other works, where they are largely hidden from public view. On the other hand, in pre-grouping days the Midland was very secretive about what went on behind the closed doors, and entrance to the forbidden precincts was about as easy as it would be to the Kremlin, whereas most other railways were prepared to receive occasional parties of visitors. For this reason very few people were fortunate enough even to catch a glimpse of the Paget 2-6-2 which was built in 1908 and made very few public appearances. Even the renowned large engine for the Lickey Incline remained much of an enigma, no details having been released before it first appeared on New Year's Day, 1920, on which occasion the author, by great good fortune, happened to be there and was able to obtain surreptitiously what was probably the first photograph taken of it (plate p 44).

The Midland station also regularly saw engines of the LNWR and NSR on through trains from Walsall and Stoke. Locomotives from the associated M&GNJR and S&DJR occasionally turned up, but otherwise in pre-grouping days 'foreigners' were exceedingly rare. After 1923 other constituents of the LMS made their appearance, L&YR occasionally, and even Caledonian and G&SWR, whereas during the second world war all sorts of strangers were seen: LNER, LSWR, and SE&CR (some Stirling 4-4-0s being stationed there for a time).

On its westward extension from Nottingham, the Great Northern had its own station, Friargate, at the other end of the town but had no physical connection whatever with the Midland. This was most unusual in a large town or city served by two or more railways, as interchange facilities of some sort were normal.

The GNR line through Derby, which crossed over the Midland at the northern end of the town, is now closed, but from Friargate to Egginton Junction (where it joined with the North Stafford) the line is being used for high-speed-train research purposes.

An artist's impression of Derby station in North Midland Railway days.

Exterior of Derby station as first built.

New 0-10-0 No 2290 running its first trials at Derby on New Year's Day 1920.

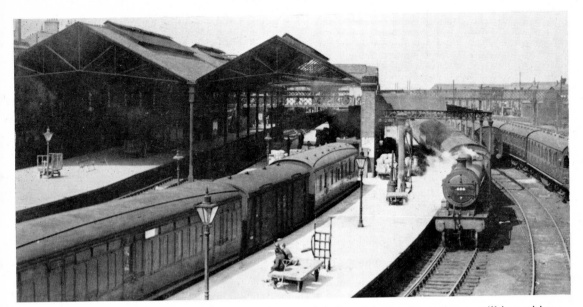

The south end of Derby station in 1946, when two spans of the original train shed were still in position.

The engine sidings opposite the station were usually full of easily visible locomotives, although many others could only be seen in the distance and were maddeningly inaccessible. This view shows the original roundhouse, now demolished.

An old view of the interior of one of the later twin roundhouses.

North end of Derby station in 1950 with a Caprotti 4-6-0- No 44747 leaving for Leeds.

Derby Friargate, GNR station, in 1933.

IMPORTANT RAILWAY CENTRES— BIRMINGHAM

Birmingham was served by three important trunk routes: the LNWR from London to Wolverhampton and Stafford, the Midland from Leeds to Bristol, and the GWR from London to Chester. The original London & Birmingham terminus was at Curzon Street, used also by the Birmingham & Gloucester Railway from 1841 until the opening in 1854 of New Street, thenceforth shared by the LNWR and Midland. The Birmingham & Derby Junction reached Hampton in 1839 and Lawley Street in 1842, and after incorporation with the Midland in 1844, became part of the through route between Derby and Bristol. New Street was thenceforth one of the two principal stations in Birmingham, the other being the Great Western one at Snow Hill. Under recent 'rationalisation', whereby the GWR main line trains terminate at Birmingham, these have been diverted to New Street and the pleasant, commodious station at Snow Hill practically closed altogether.

New Street was divided into two parts, one for the LNWR and one for the Midland, and has been completely rebuilt and modernised in the last few years, whether or not for the better being a matter of opinion. The approaches were through tunnels, and although in steam days it was liable to be somewhat smokey, the train shed was at least fairly lofty. The new low roof with its somewhat claustrophobic effect, whilst being suitable for electric working, is hardly so for the diesels which form at least fifty per cent of the traffic, and the fumes are liable to become somewhat overpowering at times. Apart from this, there are now no amenities, not even lavatories, at platform level. Indeed, one is lucky to find an unoccupied platform seat, whereas there used to be waiting rooms and a refreshment room. For all these one now has to ascend to the upper regions. Nevertheless there is a higher standard of cleanliness, well suited to the frequent fast electric services.

All three railways used to have a busy local service to the outlying districts of Birmingham, but most of this, the shorter distance traffic in particular, has now either shrunk severely or disappeared entirely.

Restored compound No 1000 with a special train to York and Doncaster, 30 August 1959.

New Street station, Midland side, April 1958, showing a MR Johnson 4-4-0, rebuilt by Deeley, No 40501.

New Street, south end, showing a train to Redditch on the left with 2-6-4T No 42340, and to Malvern Wells on right with 4-6-0 No 44814.

New Street station in 1910.

New Street station in 1968.

This spacious GWR station at Snow Hill is now virtually closed, most train services having been diverted to New Street.

Another view of New Street: June 1958, a Bournemouth-Cleethorpes train with BI No 61374. LNER engines were rarely seen in Birmingham.

A stranger to the GWR station, 24 February 1962: LMS 'Baby Scot' No 45504 **Royal Signals** with a local to Wolverhampton.

Southampton-Birmingham football excursion climbing through Old Hill station, 27 April 1963, headed by LMS 2-8-0 No 48430 and SR 'West Country' No 34046 **Braunton**.

Nameplate of Pacific No 6235.

Wolverhampton High Level station in pre-grouping days.

IMPORTANT RAILWAY CENTRES—CREWE

Crewe—almost a household word, not only to the railway traveller but to the general public, even if they have never been near the place, or have rarely or never travelled by train. From Crewe's one and only station one could, and still can, travel in one of many directions towards all parts of the country, a distinction shared to a lesser extent only by a few other centres such as Derby, York and Carlisle.

Before the coming of railways Crewe was just a remote hamlet, but gradually it evolved into a busy industrial town with reputedly the largest railway works in the world. Over 7,000 locomotives were built there; the 2,000 mark was passed as early as 1876, 4,000 in 1900. The engine concerned, a Webb four-cylinder compound 4-4-0 **La France** suitably carried the number 4000 for a time, although it was really No 1926; similarly, eleven years later, **Coronation** carried the number 5000. When the 7000th engine appeared in 1950, a BR Ivatt tank No 41272, it was little thought that the era of steam was shortly to come to an end and that there would never be an 8000.

Interior of Crewe station about 1918.

North end of Crewe, showing the old footbridge leading to the works.

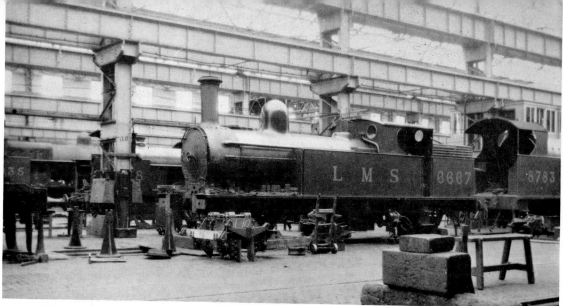

Interior of Crewe works, 1931.

A sight no longer to be seen; two new engines outshopped in works grey, August 1953. These were standard 2-6-2Ts Nos 84008 and 84009, the last new tank engine design to be introduced by BR.

The first engine built at Crewe, in 1845, No 49 **Columbine.** Between 1877 and 1902 it was transferred to the Engineers' Department in North Wales and ran as **Engineer Bangor,** as shown in the illustration. Now preserved in York Museum.

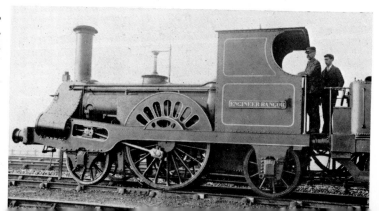

54

The 5000th engine built at Crewe Works in 1911.

Commemorative plaque on the 7000th engine built at Crewe Works, Ivatt 2-6-2T No 41272.

The end of the road. A line of engines in the cutting-up shed, May 1947. Coal tank No. 7722 is already partly stripped.

IMPORTANT RAILWAY CENTRES— NOTTINGHAM

In 1839 Nottingham was first reached from Derby by the Midland Counties Railway. This isolated section was joined to the main Leicester to Rugby line in 1840, the junction being at the point later known as Trent when the station there was opened in 1862. In 1844 the MCR amalgamated with the North Midland and the Birmingham & Derby to become the nucleus of the Midland Railway. The Midland extended the Nottingham line eastwards to Lincoln in 1846, thus penetrating the area which was to become mainly Great Northern territory. This latter railway in time reached Nottingham over the erstwhile line from Grantham. Originally an independent concern with the ambitious title of Ambergate, Nottingham & Boston & Eastern Junction Railway, its first attempt to exercise its disputed running powers into the MR station resulted in its engine being impounded by the Midland and locked up in a shed. This occurred on 2 August 1852; the engine was released five days later. As a result, the GNR built its own station at London Road adjacent to the MR. Subsequent disputes with the Midland led to the GNR continuing its own line from Colwick westwards towards Derby, but only by a circuitous route round the north of the city.

It was not until the MS&LR extended itself to London in the 1890s and became the Great Central that Nottingham's other principal station came into being. Built jointly by the GNR and GCR, it was a fine station in the heart of the city centre. Its construction involved an immense excavation of rock, and it was approached at either end by a tunnel. It was opened on 24 May 1900. The recent closure of the Great Central main line and the Great Northern Derby line has resulted in the complete closure of Victoria station, the only remaining GNR passenger service being diverted to the Midland station, as the Great Northern had attempted to do well over a century ago.

Nottingham Midland station still retains considerable importance. Through trains from St Pancras to Leeds and Scotland, which used to run via Melton Mowbray have recently been diverted over the main line through Leicester, so now have to reverse at Nottingham.

No account of railways in the Nottingham area would be complete without reference to that curiosity of the Midlands, Trent station, from where it was possible to travel either south to London or north to Manchester or Leeds, setting off in either direction and from either of the two sides of its single island platform. It must have been very confusing for the casual and uninitiated traveller changing at this junction and finding that he had to take a train proceeding in the opposite direction from that expected; this can only be made clear by examination of the accompanying diagram. Trent station was almost entirely an interchange point with very little local traffic; unfortunately 'was' is the operative word as it has recently been closed and demolished.

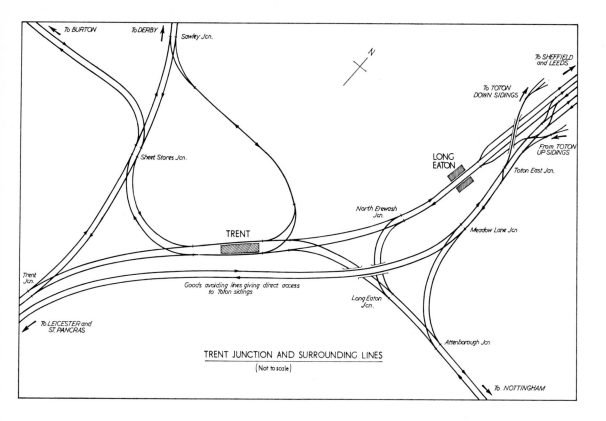

TRENT JUNCTION AND SURROUNDING LINES
(Not to scale)

Trent, east junction. The line to Nottingham is straight ahead; the middle lines run to Toton, Chesterfield and the north, and the single branch to the left swings round to rejoin the main line from Leicester to Derby, enabling a train between these two points to make a diversionary call at Trent, with the object of giving a connection to Nottingham.

Nottingham MR station in 1947. The overbridge carried the GCR main line.

Floods at Nottingham, 19 March 1947.

GCR A5 4-6-2T at Nottingham Victoria 1950. This view well illustrates the extensive rock excavation which was necessary to build the station, which is flanked by a tunnel at each end.

Victoria Station in its later and declining days. This view, taken in 1962, shows 'Britannia' No 70049 **Solway Firth** from London on one of the few GCR trains surviving at that time.

Weekday Cross Junction: GCR main line to the south is on the right, GNR line to Grantham on the left. These lines have been abandoned with the closure of Victoria station.

LEICESTER AND OTHER CENTRES

Other important railway towns or centres which come within the prescribed area hardly warrant a complete chapter to themselves, but may now be dealt with in one section. Chief among these is Leicester, whose first railway, the Leicester & Swannington, is alluded to in Chapter 1. From a main line point of view, Leicester was first reached by the Midland Counties Railway from Derby in 1840. The line extended southwards to Rugby, where it linked up with the London & Birmingham. It was over this route that the Midland was first able to reach London.

The opening of the GCR London extension in 1899 gave Leicester a second important main line, and a new station. Although not so large and commodious as the Midland one which had just been entirely rebuilt, it was nevertheless a worthy affair. Until but a few years ago, who could have forecast that this important station, complete with refreshment room, would have been reduced to an unstaffed halt. Its only present function is a place of call for the pitiful service of diesel multiple units over the only remnant now remaining of the former GCR main line, which not so long ago boasted such fine express trains as the 'Master Cutler'.

Leicester did in fact have another somewhat pretentious though lesser known station, Belgrave Road, a terminal owned by the Great Northern, on what was little more than a country branch line. The two large overall spans and four commodious platforms can rarely if ever have been used to capacity except possibly on a few busy Saturdays in the summer, when through trains were run to east coast resorts. The line is now completely closed.

Rugby was first reached by the London & Birmingham Railway in 1838 and by the Midland Counties in 1840, which year may therefore be said to mark the beginning of Rugby's importance as a railway junction. The opening of the Trent Valley line between Rugby and Stafford in 1847 was partly aimed at relieving Birmingham of some of the through traffic to the north, but more particularly at shortening the distance between London and Manchester and Liverpool. In 1850 branches were opened from Rugby to Stamford, passing through Market Harborough, and a year later the line to Leamington was opened.

Rugby became second in importance only to Crewe on the LNWR main line, and many of the principal trains of the day called there. After the amalgamation of 1923 the LMS and the LNER established a locomotive testing plant which was used by many of the most famous locomotives in the country. Dickens wrote with extraordinary perception about 'Mugby Junction', which was obviously Rugby, and perhaps his most accurate description is in *The Lazy Tour of Two Idle Apprentices*; almost everything is included, from the signalman 'drawing immense quantities of beer', to the glaring gas-lit advertisements on the station walls.

It may be mentioned that the present LNWR station at Rugby was not completed until 1886; there had previously been two others. The GCR extension to Rugby gave the town its second existing station, somewhat remotely situated on the southern outskirts, although rather misleadingly called Rugby Central. It is now the terminal point of the diesel railcar service from Nottingham.

Further north, the important industrial city of Sheffield was served by two principal main lines; the old North Midland, and the Manchester, Sheffield & Lincolnshire. These became respectively the Midland and the Great Central, and at the grouping, the LMS and the LNER. Until 1870 when the direct line from Chesterfield via Dore was opened, Sheffield had been served by a branch from Rotherham. After nationalisation, when the concept of dividing the whole railway system into geographical regions rather than through routes, which one would have considered more logical and practical for a transport concern, was put forward, Sheffield presented the problem which arose in many areas and towns (Birmingham was of course another) where two principal railways from what were hitherto different regions had to be reconciled into one. Sheffield was designated as 'Eastern Region', thus chopping the Midland main line, for operating purposes, into two different areas. This difficulty has arisen elsewhere throughout the country, and has never been satisfactorily solved.

Chesterfield, although not quite in the category of an important centre, is interesting in that it was served by three railways. The Midland had been there since very early days, but in the 1890s two further lines were promoted, both of which would reach Chesterfield. These were the GCR London extension, and the independent Lancashire, Derbyshire & East Coast Railway, an ambitious project which never got anywhere near either Lancashire or the east coast.

The particularly interesting feature in the lay-out of the lines in the town is that the three railways concerned cross one another at one point in three tiers, one above the other, well illustrated in the accompanying photograph. An LD&ECR train is seen on the upper viaduct, the new GCR main line is in the cutting, and between the two runs the Midland.

A very similar lay-out is to be found in the USA at Richmond, Virginia, and these are possibly the only two such examples in the world. The LD&ECR was absorbed by the Great Central in 1907, but both of its routes in Chesterfield have now been abandoned, leaving only the original North Midland Railway.

The unique situation of Chesterfield's three railways, the GCR loop line of the London Extension in the foreground, crossed by the Midland main line (the original North Midland Railway), whilst above runs a train on the Lancashire, Derbyshire & East Coast Railway. Of these three railways only the MR now survives and the lofty viaduct has been demolished.

Lastly, Lincoln, at the eastern end of the area. Lincoln lies at the intersection of three important main lines: the old Manchester Sheffield & Lincolnshire, the Great Northern line from Peterborough through Boston, and the Great Northern and Great Eastern joint line, the principal artery between the eastern counties and Yorkshire. Until April 1906 the MS&LR trains used the Midland station, but were then transferred to the Great Northern into which the trains of the LD&ECR just referred to, also ran. The Midland (the first railway to reach Lincoln, which it did in 1846, two years before the GNR) had its own station close by, mainly used as a terminal.

The Midland main line at Leicester, looking south. The view was taken in 1922, and some laid off single-wheelers can be seen in sidings outside the shed.

Leicester Central, the Great Central station, in 1947. B1 4-6-0 No 1153 is seen entering with the London express.

Rugby, south end. A LNWR 'Claughton' leaves for London, whilst a train on the GCR main line passes overhead.

An old view of Stafford, looking north. The station has recently been completely rebuilt in connection with the electrification.

Most of the principal, privately owned locomotive builders were to be found in the north of England or in Scotland, but the firm of Bagnalls had their works at Stafford. Over the years they built a great many engines, mainly for industrial use. They specialised in narrow-gauge but sometimes built engines for main line use and for overseas buyers. The illustration is from one of their official specifications.

Hull & Barnsley 4-4-0 No 33 at Sheffield Midland in 1910. This railway worked a through train between Hull and Sheffield between 1 October 1905 and 1 January 1917.

Sheffield Victoria in 1947. The engines are GCR 'Director' No 2654 and North Eastern B16 4-6-0 No 1405.

The Hull & Barnsley service to Barnsley was provided by connections over the Midland from Cudworth, and one of these trains, a two coach rail motor with L&Y 2-4-2T No 50650, is seen here in 1955 at Chapeltown South.

The Midland was the first railway to reach Lincoln; this view shows the old terminus. The overall roof has now been removed.

Lincoln GNR at about the turn of the century, with a LD&ECR train entering, hauled by 0-4-4T No 18 (later GCR No 1152B).

The image of B1 No 1193 is reflected in the water; in the background can be seen Lincoln Cathedral.

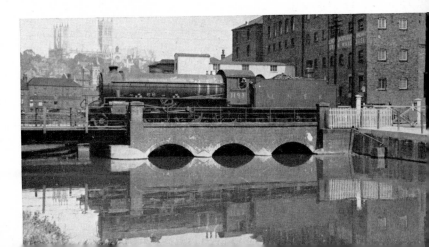

THE EREWASH VALLEY LINE

To be geographically accurate, the designation 'Erewash Valley' can only be held to apply to the stretch of line between Trent and Pye Bridge, at which point the river Erewash parts company with the railway to the north. From a railway aspect, however, the term Erewash Valley Line is more generally understood to refer loosely to the whole of the Midland main line between Trent or Nottingham, at least as far north as Chesterfield. The section from Long Eaton Junction to Pye Bridge (originally a branch terminating at Pinxton) was opened as far as Codnor Park in 1847, extended to Pye Bridge in 1849, and to Clay Cross in 1862 where it joined the original North Midland main line from Derby to Masboro'.

This area contains one of the richest coal deposits in the country, and is strewn with innumerable collieries. The Midland had a monopoly of this business until 1875 when it was challenged by the Great Northern who pushed westwards from Nottingham to tap some of the lucrative traffic, and later still, to a limited extent, by the Great Central. In the Leen Valley, a little to the east, all three railways, the MR, GNR and GCR, had lines running almost parallel and crossing one another in several places.

The GNR route, which had been opened in 1881, was officially known as the Leen Valley Line although the MR had always been the predominant railway in the area. The Erewash Valley line in particular is a very busy one as not only does it carry an enormous, although nowadays diminishing, amount of coal traffic, but it is also part of the main line from London to Leeds and Carlisle; its four tracks carry a constant stream of trains of all sorts. From a speed point of view it has always been much bedevilled by permanent way restrictions made necessary by the danger of subsidence due to the numerous colliery workings in the area.

Coal train near Chesterfield in 1911. The engine was the earliest surviving Kirtley goods, No 2300, a veteran of 1850. The famous twisted church spire can be seen in the background.

Typical coal train of the 1920s in the Erewash Valley. Kirtley 0-6-0 No 2706 and class 4 goods No 3904.

'Garratt' No 47969 near Clay Cross, 1957. Note a new industrial saddle tank, probably for use at a colliery, next to the engine.

Class 4 goods No 3970, near Langley Mill, 1946.

DERBY—CHINLEY—DORE AND TOTLEY

As previously mentioned, the centre of England comprises extreme contrasts in the variety of the scenery and surroundings, from the drab industrial areas, through much pleasant countryside, to some of the most beautiful scenery in the whole of England. The Midland main line from Derby to Manchester comes within the last category. It has sometimes been referred to as 'the Switzerland of England'. It is (or unfortunately was, for the loveliest section has recently been closed) probably the finest main line south of the border, equalled only by the wild grandeur of the same Midland Railway's line between Settle and Carlisle, also threatened with extinction.

We are concerned only with the section between Derby and Chinley; north of that point the railway comes more within the area of north-west England, but the line between Chinley and Dore and Totley, which forms part of the through route between Manchester and Sheffield, does also come into the present picture.

The Midland had long had its eyes on Manchester. The obvious direct route from its own system was over the Peak district, but this would inevitably be of difficult construction involving severe gradients and tunnelling. Eventually this project was actually achieved by extending the Manchester, Buxton & Midland Junction from its terminus at Rowsley. At Cromford it met the Cromford & High Peak line which is dealt with further in Chapter 17.

The Manchester, Buxton & Midland Junction Railway, a somewhat grandiose title, had been opened in 1849, but was worked from the start by the Midland. The branch from Millers Dale to Buxton did not materialise until 1863. The cross connection of the Manchester line with the original North Midland Railway between Chinley and Dore and Totley was also a very picturesque one, and was only constructed with much difficulty. Its passage under the Pennines necessitated two of the longest tunnels on the Midland system, Totley tunnel, 3 miles 946 yds, and Cowburn, 2 miles 182 yds, the former being the second longest in the British Isles, exceeded only by the Severn. This line was opened for freight traffic in 1893 and for passengers in 1894, and constituted one of the two principal rail links between Manchester and Sheffield, the other being the GCR route through Woodhead where, incidentally, are found Britain's fourth longest tunnels, 3 miles 313 yds.

The up York express near Duffield, with 2-4-0 No 194 and 4-4-0 No 400.

A freight train near Duffield headed by 0-6-0s Nos 3391 and 2835.

Kirtley goods No 2777 in the picturesque setting of England's 'Little Switzerland'.

Excursion train near Miller's Dale leaving Clee Tor tunnel on Easter Monday, 1956.

Compound 1024 with the down Manchester express at Miller's Dale Junction in 1932.

Another view of Blackwell Mill, Miller's Dale in 1932, showing a freight train with class 4 goods No 4043.

Class 3 goods No 3662 at Peak Forest summit, 1933.

Dore & Totley tunnel, second longest in the British Isles, 3 miles 946 yd, on the Midland direct route between Manchester and Sheffield.

Britain's fourth longest tunnels, 3 miles 313 yd, are through the same Pennine range, on the old Great Central, also between Manchester and Sheffield. This view, taken in 1947, shows a Great Northern 'Atlantic' leaving one of the original tunnels, now closed and replaced by two new adjacent bores to accommodate electric working.

THE LICKEY INCLINE

The Birmingham & Gloucester Railway, which eventually formed part of the Midland's through main line from Derby to Bristol, was opened in 1840. The contour of the country through which it passed necessitated a sharp rise over two miles, resulting in what was one of the steepest inclines on any main line in the British Isles, the gradient being 1 in 37.7. Banking assistance was an essential from the start, and has remained so ever since, although with more limited application in recent years with the coming of diesel traction.

Amongst the Birmingham & Gloucester's first engines were some 4-2-0s imported from the USA, and one of their duties was to help the light trains of those days up the incline, although it was soon necessary to supersede them with more powerful locomotives. It was not, as is sometimes stated, one of the Norris engines whose boiler exploded on 10 November 1840, killing the driver and fireman, but another locomotive, **Eclipse,** which was being tried out. The tombstones of the unfortunate driver and fireman, still to be seen in Bromsgrove Churchyard, depict one of the American engines; no doubt the mason who inscribed the stones had no drawing of the offending engine which he could copy.

The working of this incline, a busy main line on which express trains have to be intermingled with innumerable slow freights, has always presented a problem to the operating department. On a normal weekday it would be necessary for at least five banking engines to be in continuous service, some trains requiring the assistance of two or even three of them, and by the time they had reached the summit and returned to Bromsgrove their turn would probably again be near, leaving little time for taking on water and general servicing. For many years prior to 1920 the usual type to be employed was the Midland 0-6-0T of the final 1899-1902 series, the '1900s' or '7200s' as they later became. In 1920 there appeared the famous 0-10-0, No 2290 from Derby works, which earned the nickname **Big Bertha.** It was the only engine of its kind and was not only the largest the MR ever built, but only the second ten-wheeled coupled engine in these islands (the first having been the abortive and short lived GER 'Decapod', **Big Bertha** satisfactorily performed her duties for thirty-six years; one cannot attempt to calculate how many tens of thousands of times she must have pounded her way up to Blackwell. The blast from her four cylinders made a magnificent sound, fortunately, thanks to the activities of Mr Peter Handford, preserved for all time on an Argo record.

After the grouping, the stud of engines was mainly the improved 0-6-0Ts latterly known as 'Jinties'; other types were tried out, usually unsuccessfully, amongst which may be mentioned a LNWR 0-8-4T. Unfortunately no photograph appears to have been taken, or at any rate to have survived, of the experiment.

The LNER six-cylinder Garratt, rendered redundant by the electrification of the Worsborough incline in 1950 (see next chapter), also joined **Big Bertha** for a time, but for some reason was not very much liked. When the MR 0-10-0 was withdrawn in 1956 it was replaced by a standard Class 9 2-10-0 No 92079. Since 1920 the policy had been to provide one large engine together with several smaller ones, but the exact economics of this practice are not very apparent. No discrimination was made between the two types and all took their turn strictly in rotation whatever kind of train had to be assisted.

When Bromsgrove became part of the Western Region some 0-6-0PTs of GWR design gradually replaced the LMS types, and a GWR 2-8-0T was also used for a time. These eventually gave way to English Electric type 3 diesels, in turn more recently replaced by 'Hymeks'.

Train ascending the Lickey Incline behind one of Kirtley's '170' class 2-4-0s, built by Beyer Peacock in 1867.

Another view, taken in 1911. The train engines are Johnson single-wheeler No 630 and 2-4-0 No 197.

View in 1911 of a train near the summit, banked by 0-6-0T No 1933 and one of the earlier Kirtley straight framed 0-6-0s, which dated back to 1850-1863.

Class '2' 4-4-0 No 513 commencing the ascent of the Incline just after passing through Bromsgrove station.

An early picture of 0-10-0 No 2290, at the top of the Incline, soon after she was built in 1920.

An unuaual view of **Big Bertha** and the Garratt together at Bromsgrove, May 1949.

An impressive close-up of the 0-10-0 banking a train in 1955, the rear coach being an LNER observation car.

Bromsgrove engine sidings and coal stage for the bankers, January 1957, showing GWR Pannier No 8402 and 2-10-0 No 92079, which had replaced **Big Bertha.**

View from the rear of a train in Bromsgrove station, 1963. No 8401 is running up to give banking assistance.

Another view from the rear of a train, this time at the summit at Blackwell in September 1959, GWR 2-8-0T No 5226 is dropping off after banking.

THE WORSBOROUGH INCLINE

The Worsborough Incline near Barnsley in South Yorkshire, although not on a main line in the sense that it never had a passenger service, is nevertheless on a most important link of the old Manchester, Sheffield & Lincolnshire Railway. It carries through freight traffic between Lancashire and the important maze of lines around Mexboro' and Doncaster, a particular point of concentration being the large marshalling yard at Wath built by the Great Central.

Leaving the Barnsley branch at Silkstone Junction, the divergence avoids Barnsley and rejoins the main line at Wentworth Junction, near Wombwell, a distance of nine miles. The land drops several hundred feet in this distance; consequently west bound trains have the gradient—1 in 40 in places— almost exclusively against them, necessitating the use of bankers for the heavy coal trains. It was for this job that Gresley built his 2-8-8-2 Garratt in 1925, the largest and most powerful engine ever to work in this country. It spent almost the whole of its working life on this duty, but when the line was electrified in 1950, the Garratt was transferred to the Lickey Incline (see previous chapter) for a time before being finally withdrawn. Normally five bankers were necessary as the traffic was heavy and continuous, most trains requiring two additional engines. Even the Garratt needed the assistance of a second helper on some trains. The supplementary engines, supplied from Mexboro' shed, were usually Great Central 2-8-0s or 0-8-0s and, latterly some WD austerity 2-8-0s. Some trains even had a pilot engine at the front, making four engines in all. There are two short tunnels near the top of the bank, and with three or four engines pounding their way up, the atmosphere was unbelievable. It was necessary to place some sort of pad over one's face to make breathing at all possible, but all this has of course vanished since the electric locomotives took over.

Gresley's Garratt, built in 1925 for working the Worsboro' Incline; the most powerful steam engine to run in these islands. It was virtually two 2-8-0s built into one. This interesting early view shows it running trials soon after construction.

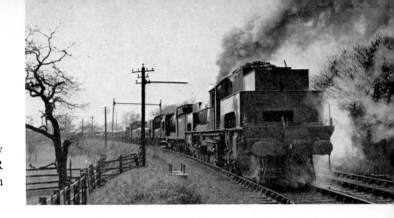

A later view of the Gresley Garratt, now renumbered 9999, together with a GCR 2-8-0, battling its way up the Incline in 1946.

GCR 0-8-0 No 3219 tackling the bank, the smoke from the banking engine can be seen in the background.

Trains on the Worsboro' bank are now operated entirely by electric locomotives of the type illustrated by this view of No 26030 at Penistone.

THE CROMFORD & HIGH PEAK RAILWAY

This remote and, before the days of motor cars, somewhat inaccessible line, was an early and ambitious project to construct a railway over the wild moorlands of the Derbyshire Peak District with the object of providing a direct route between the agricultural and mineral country around Derby and the large industrial area around Manchester.

The original idea was for the construction of a waterway connecting the already existing Cromford Canal (opened in 1792) and the Peak Forest Canal (1800), by-passing the worst of the intervening high ground with a route via Chesterfield and Bugsworth. Even this project would have entailed a large number of locks to reach the summit levels, coupled with a difficulty of maintaining the necessary water supply in a somewhat arid limestone district.

In 1823, therefore, the decision was made to construct a railway, the route being surveyed by the engineer, Josiah Jessop. Amongst the subscribers to the scheme were Richard Arkwright and Lord Anson. The Cromford & High Peak Railway, as it was incorporated under an Act of 1825, was opened from Cromford Wharf to Hurdlow in 1830 and from Hurdlow to Whaley Bridge in 1831. It antedated the Leicester & Swannington, referred to in Chapter 1, but as it was initially worked by horses it cannot lay claim to being the first line in the Midlands operated with steam locomotives—these came on the scene later. It was however one of the earliest railways of any considerable length for it stretched nearly thirty-four miles. From Cromford Wharf, situated at the terminus of the Cromford Canal (which linked up with the Nottingham, Derby & Trent and Mersey Canals) there was initially a steeply inclined plane with gradients of 1 in 8 and 1 in 9 to a first summit at Sheeppasture, and after a short level section there was a second incline at Middleton, with a gradient of 1 in 8¼. In this distance of about four miles the line rose between 900 and 1000 ft. The summit of the railway, which occurs at Ladmanlow near the other end of the line, attains a maximum of 1265 ft above sea level.

These two inclines, both double tracked so that the benefit of partial balancing of weights can be obtained by operating ascending and decending wagons simultaneously, were worked by beam engines, the one at Middleton being of special interest in that it dates from 1825, possibly the oldest still at work when the line finally closed.

From Middleton Top the line is comparatively level, apart from one further incline 457 yds long at 1 in 60, 1 in 30, 1 in 20 and the final 200 yds at 1 in 14. This also was first operated with the winding engine, but from 1877 onwards it was worked by orthodox locomotives, being the steepest gradient in the country to be so worked. Even so, this was only possible by taking a run at the incline; 60 mph was often attained until an accident in 1937, after which a limit of 40 mph was imposed, entailing a reduction of load from five to four wagons. Usually the engine just managed to reach the top, but if not, a second 'charge' had to be made. This line continued over the wild moorland and eventually, by means of more descending inclines, reached Whaley Bridge where it made contact with the Peak Forest Canal.

One section, between Parsley Hay and Hurdlow, eventually became part of the LNWR branch from Buxton to Ashbourne. Beyond Hurdlow the original alignment of the C&HPR was abandoned to Harpur Hill and the trains ran over the newer branch. None of the original C&HPR now remains in operation, the last section, between Parsley Hay and Friden, being finally closed in October 1967.

The comparatively level sections between the inclines were at first worked by horses, but trials with locomotives were made in 1834 and steam locomotives completely replaced the old form of motive power in 1841, except for a short section at Whaley Bridge which was horse-worked until its closure in 1952. Most of the line beyond Ladmanlow had been abandoned as long ago as 1892.

Until 1861 when the line was taken over by the LNWR, the C&HPR possessed its own stud of locomotives and an odd collection they were. Thereafter the LNWR used its own engines, mostly old 'Crewe goods' types, but various strangers appeared at times, amongst which was the Sandy & Potton **Shannon.** later acquired by the Wantage Tramway, and now preserved. In later days the motive power was principally LNWR 2-4-0Ts (known as 'Choppers'), followed in more recent times by North London 0-6-0Ts, and latterly by LMS 0-4-0ST No 47000 and MR 0-4-0T No 41536. Last of all came the austerity 0-6-0STs of the LNER J94 type.

Although in view of the inclines, the line was really quite unsuited for the conveyance of passenger traffic, attempts were made to provide some sort of service and as early as 1833 a daily passenger train was run through from Middleton Top to Whaley Bridge, with a coach connection to Manchester, seats being booked through in both directions: probably the earliest instance of through rail/road bookings. Passengers had to walk up and down the inclines and the service ceased in 1877.

How such a line ever came to be built may well be asked; the sparsely populated countryside would hardly seem to have warranted the construction of a railway, even in those days. However, apart from the original intention of forming part of a through route between Derbyshire and Lancashire, there was also a healthy quarrying industry and a number of small farms and hamlets. Water was extremely scarce in the region, and was supplied by the railway in specially adapted water tanks which were hauled up the incline from Cromford.

Since the final closure in 1967 the site of the railway has been bought by the Derbyshire County Council with the object of converting it to a hikers' footpath.

Cromford & High Peak No 4, built in 1860, either by Bury or the Vulcan Foundry. The saddle tank was added later at Cromford. On being taken over by the LNWR in 1871 it was sent to Crewe as a works shunter and became 'D' in the service list. Scrapped May 1882.

An old view of a train on the C&HPR with a 'Crewe goods' 2-4-0.

A train, headed by a North London 0-6-0T No 7527, ascending Hopton Incline in 1934, at the point where the gradient stiffens from 1-in-30 to the final 1-in-14.

The bottom of Sheeppasture Incline, with water tank (accompanied by workman with bicycle) ascending. The runaway catch pit can be seen through the bridge.

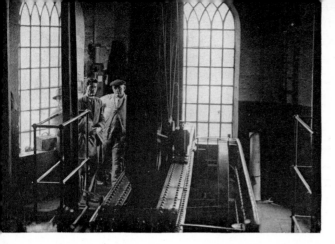

The old winding engine at Middleton Incline, built by the Butterley Company in 1825, and in use until the recent closure of the line.

North London 0-6-0T, No 27530, in 1940.

Parsley Hay station and Junction, looking south. The LNWR Ashbourne branch is to the right, the original C&HPR continues straight ahead.

EARLY TRAMROADS AND PLATEWAYS

In the same part of the country as the Cromford & High Peak Railway just described, was another, even older, line built with much the same idea in mind: that of making a link over the High Peak hills from Manchester eastwards, in this case to north Derbyshire and the Sheffield area. It was originally planned as a canal, and the first section of it was actually built as such. However from Bugsworth, an important inland canal basin around the turn of the eighteenth century, the terrain was considered unsuitable for a canal and so the Peak Forest Tramway came into being, running in a south-easterly direction to the extensive lime quarries around Dove Holes. It was opened in 1799, and was one of the earliest through tramroads, or plateways, using cast iron rails, in the country.* During its 128 years of existence it never employed any motive power other than horses. The general contour of the line was a gradually ascending one, with an inclined plane 512 yds long in the centre section. As the gradient was in favour of the descending loaded wagons this could be rope worked, with a controlling brake drum at the top. The line, which was $6\frac{1}{2}$ miles long, rose some 625 ft in all, with a summit 1,158 ft above sea level. It was last used in 1926 and the track lifted, but the course of the line can still be followed in places. The line was at one time leased to the Manchester, Sheffield & Lincolnshire Railway, coming into that company's full control in 1863 and passing in time to the Great Central and the LNER.

Another very early plateway, near Derby itself, was a line from Little Eaton to Kilburn and Denby, built in 1795 (the later Midland Railway Ripley branch followed more or less the same course) and in use until 1908. It was known as the little Eaton Gangway.

A little further south is Ashby-de-la-Zouch where the Ashby Canal had thirty miles of lock-free waterway with twenty miles of connecting tramways radiating into the Leicester coalfields. The canal was sold in 1846 to the Midland Railway and some of the beds were subsequently used for railway construction. One of the branches was the Ticknall Tramroad, with the unusual gauge of 4 ft 2 in, and after the Ashby to Melbourne line was opened it ran to Ticknall with a branch to Dinsdale Quarry, a distance of four and a half miles. The last trip was on 20 May 1913.

*The cast iron edge rail is thought to have been first introduced in 1789 at Loughborough.

Peak Forest canal basin and tramway sidings at Bugsworth in 1927.

Peak Forest Tramway track, switch and wagon.

The Denby plateway at Coxbench.

Ticknall Tramroad, Ashby-de-la-Zouch canal. This picture is of the biannual trip to establish right of way. The last journey was made in May 1913.

Old Stratford & Moreton Tramway wagon, preserved at Stratford-on-Avon in Bancroft Gardens, near the theatre. The cast-iron edge rail is thought to have been first used at Loughboro' in 1789.

THE LEEK & MANIFOLD VALLEY LIGHT RAILWAY AND CALDON LOW TRAMWAY

Few counties in Britain can show such a complete contrast in scenic surroundings as may be found in Staffordshire which by no stretch of imagination can be held to be one of the most attractive of English counties. It is only the fifteenth largest, but comes seventh in population, embracing the Potteries and the Black Country around Wolverhampton, together with other industrial areas. Yet at its north-east corner, where the southern ends of the Peak District intrude from neighbouring Derbyshire, lies the beautiful valley of the Dove. Although only some fifteen miles from the smoking kilns and furnaces of Stoke-on-Trent, this is one of the most unspoiled areas still remaining in England and fortunately much of it is in the hands of the National Trust.

In direct contrast with the rest of the county, this district is sparsely populated and largely agricultural, most farmers concentrate on milk production for the nature of the soil precludes much in the way of arable farming. In the circumstances it is not surprising that railway development in the area bounded by the North Stafford line between Burton and Macclesfield on the west and the LNWR Ashbourne to Buxton line to the east, was non-existent until the end of the nineteenth century.

The passing of the Light Railways Act in 1896, however, opened the way for the construction of a narrow-gauge line, nine miles in length, from Waterhouses up the Manifold Valley to a terminus at Hulme End. Connection was made to the main railway system with the construction by the NSR of a new branch from Cheddleton to Waterhouses. The Leek & Manifold Valley Light Railway was a separate company, but was worked from the start by the NSR and, at the grouping passed into the hands of the LMS. A spur of the new standard-gauge line at Waterhouses gave the NSR better access to the valuable limestone deposits in a quarry at Caldon Low.

The L&MVLR was constructed to the unusual gauge of 2 ft 6 in and, although it was originally the intention to reach Buxton, the line never got farther than Hulme End, which was in the open countryside, although its name was later optimistically changed to Hulme End for Sheen and Hartington. There were seven intermediate stations along the winding valley and the line was popular with tourists in the summer, but otherwise the chief traffic was for carrying milk from the surrounding farms. There was provision for the conveying of standard gauge trucks and milk tanks by the use of transporter wagons, and at one time there was a good traffic of milk tanks between the Manifold Valley and London, for they could run throughout without break of gauge. There were two 2-6-2T engines: No 1, **E. R. Calthrop,** and No 2, **J. B. Earle.** They were large for such a narrow gauge, and had enormous headlamps such as are rarely seen in this country. Today there is little left to remind one of the charming, small railway that once ran up this beautiful valley.

The line was opened in 1904 but was never a financial success, and with the gradual growth of road competition its ultimate fate was inevitable. It lingered on for a few years under LMS ownership, but was finally closed to all traffic on 12 March 1934.

The track was converted to a tarmacadamed footpath for use by pedestrians; fortunately not into a road for streams of cars to disturb the peace of the valley, although part of the site has since in fact so succumbed.

Mention should be made of the Caldon Low Quarry, already briefly alluded to. This valuable limestone quarry had in turn been served by four different tramroads from a branch of the Trent & Mersey Canal at Froghall Basin. Froghall was situated at a terminus of the old Peak Forest Canal which at one time gave through outlet to the sea at Liverpool. The original line dated back to as long ago as 1777, being in fact the second railway to be authorised in England. It was reconstructed in 1780 and abandoned in 1802 when a new plateway was built. This in turn was superseded in 1849 by another diversion, a 3 ft 6 in gauge line built by the North Stafford Railway and operated in three sections by cables and gravity. This remained in use until 1920, when the southern part of the quarry was worked out and replaced by new workings on the north side served by the NSR standard gauge off the Waterhouses branch.

An early view of the L&MVLR train showing a coach in the original yellow livery.

One of the two 2-6-2Ts built in 1904 by Messrs Kitson & Co.

Thors Cave station, 1934.

A view of the route from Thors Cave, one of the most picturesque parts of the line.

Thors Cave station in 1940, after the conversion of the trackbed into a public footpath. It was somewhat remarkable that six years after closure, the station name board should still be *in situ*. One could hardly imagine such a state of affairs in these souvenir-hunting days, when such an interesting relic would have been either officially or unofficially removed.

Transporter wagon for through conveyance of standard-gauge stock.

Waterhouses station on the new standard-gauge branch built to give access to the Leek & Manifold Valley Railway.

One of the 3ft 6in gauge Caldon Low quarry engines, **Toad,** owned by the North Stafford. The other two were **Frog** and **Bobs.**

Abandoned cable incline at Caldon Low quarries, 1933.

COLLIERY RAILWAYS

One of the most valuable mineral resources of Britain is, of course, coal, and one of the most important coalfields lies in the Midlands, chiefly in the counties of Derbyshire, Nottinghamshire, Leicestershire, Staffordshire and Warwickshire. Coal mining is now regrettably a declining industry. This is doubly unfortunate in that, whilst there are still vast deposits under our very feet, nearly all the oil which replaces it has to be imported from abroad. The number of collieries which were sunk during the nineteenth and early part of the twentieth centuries ran into three figures in the Midlands alone. Each had its own railway system, generally situated adjacent to the main railway network, and usually its own stud of shunting engines, perhaps only two in the case of the smaller pits, but several at the larger ones. Once privately owned, they have since 1947 been taken over by the National Coal Board. The engines were usually of the 0-4-0ST or 0-6-0ST types built by such firms as Manning Wardle, Hudswell Clarke, Peckett & Sons, and many others, but sometimes they were engines obtained second-hand from one of the main line companies.

Since the gradual extinction of steam on BR, an increasing interest has been taken in industrial locomotives in general, but here again they are on the decline, being in many cases replaced by the inevitable diesels. This has not generally been found so economic in collieries, where the necessary fuel is literally on the doorstep, whereas a diesel has to have its oil imported from overseas, surely a fantastic situation!

One of the very earliest colliery lines in the Midlands was the Shutt End Railway, built to convey coal from the Earl of Dudley's collieries at Wall Heath near Dudley, to the Staffordshire & Worcestershire Canal at Ashwood Basin, a distance of about two miles. The line was opened in 1829, the same year as the Liverpool & Manchester, and one of the original engines was **Agenoria,** now in York Museum. Most of the earlier locomotives were of the 0-4-0 tender design, as typified by the illustration of **Ednam,** built in 1872. All of these were scrapped many years ago.

An early engine on the Shutt End Colliery Railway.

The Cannock Chase & Wolverhampton Railway had, until a few years ago, some fine but elderly Beyer Peacock 0-4-2s, some of which were at work for about ninety years. This view shows a group of three of them; **McClean** (the oldest, dating back to 1856), **Chawner** and **Anglesey** at their shed after a day's work in 1946. Whether the hot water being drawn off **McClean** is for washing purposes or for brewing tea, cannot now be stated with any certainty.

The ultimate in colliery locomotives, a Beyer Garratt at the Baddesley Colliery, Atherstone, Warwick. This engine is now preserved at Bressingham Hall, Diss.

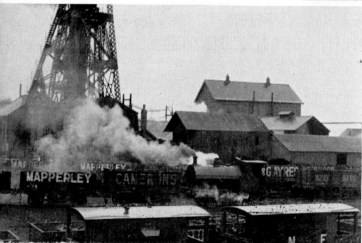

A typical colliery scene at West Hallam, Derbyshire, in 1940.

View through cab window of an old Beyer Peacock saddle tank at Rothervale Colliery in 1956.

90

Typical scene in the colliery mining village of Treeton, near Sheffield.

A striking, but little remarked upon, change in the general railway scene during the last twenty years, stems from the time when BR took over all privately owned wagons. Until then there were many such, particularly those owned by collieries, and the average freight train could present a fascinating variety of private ownerships, such as glimpsed in this picture taken in 1937.

The wooden wagon itself has now almost completely disappeared; this type was common until only a few years ago.

Works plate on a colliery wagon.

IRON ORE RAILWAYS

In the area which may broadly be described as the eastern Midlands there are immense deposits of iron ore. There is, in fact, one of the largest iron fields in Europe and it is of great importance to the economy of the country. Since 1945 about ninety-one per cent of the steel industry's annual requirement of between fifteen and twenty million tons of ore, has been won in the counties of Lincolnshire, Leicestershire, Rutland, Northamptonshire and Oxfordshire. Most of the large steel furnaces of the country are situated in the north-east, the north Midlands, and South Wales, but there is a large, fully integrated steelworks at Corby in Northants, which has its own extensive railway system, linking the surrounding quarries with its main works, and situated adjacent to the MR main line via Melton Mowbray (not now used by passenger trains). There was a smaller furnace at Kettering, west of the line a mile or two north of the station, but this has been closed and the works completely dismantled. This company had its own 3 ft-gauge line for carrying the iron ore from the nearby quarries. There was another similar ironworks at Wellingborough.

A number of other quarries were to be found dotted here and there in this otherwise entirely rural part of Northants and Leicestershire. The quarries were often well hidden so that it could come as a complete surprise, when motoring along these quiet byways, suddenly to see a small railway system with a locomotive and train of iron ore wagons making its way to a railhead on the main BR system to convey the ore to some distant steelworks. Some of these small railways were of standard gauge and others of varying narrow dimensions, but nearly all have closed within the last ten or fifteen years in favour of road transport. One of the last to close was a 3 ft 3 in system at Wellingborough which was in use until 1966. A much earlier casualty was the Edge Hill Light Railway, built during the first world war to tap a rich bed of ore situated on a high escarpment in the hills bordering north Oxfordshire and Warwickshire. This involved the construction of a steep cable-worked incline to bring the ore down to the old SMJR at Burton Dassett. The EHLR was constructed as a wartime measure when the importation of iron ore from abroad was difficult.

Traffic diminished on the cessation of hostilities and the line closed suddenly and without warning on 27 January 1925, never to be re-opened. Everything was left derelict, just as it was for a good many years afterwards, including the engines (two of Stroudley's famous LBSC 'Terriers') and a small saddle-tank which were still standing forlornly in the open as late as 1939.

The Edge Hill Light Railway in 1935, ten years after abandonment. The incline can be seen in the background.

One of the LBSC Terriers still standing forlornly in 1939, not having been moved for fourteen years.

Until recently this was a typical scene in the quiet Northamptonshire countryside. An iron ore train at Scaldwell in 1959.

The Scaldwell Ironstone Company operated two gauges, 3 ft into the quarries and standard to the BR railhead at Lamport. This view shows the transhipment stage from narrow to standard gauge.

Eastwell cable operated incline, one of the last such in the country, when this view was taken in 1959. It conveyed the iron ore from the quarries down to the main BR railhead.

OTHER INDUSTRIAL SYSTEMS

Apart from collieries, ironworks, steelworks and the iron ore fields described in the previous chapter, many other industries are to be found in the Midlands, amongst the most notable being the Potteries already referred to in the North Stafford Railway chapter. However, they had no railway system of their own, as did the very important brewing industry at Burton-on-Trent. The particular properties of the water made Burton-on-Trent exceptionally suitable for the manufacture of those very popular brews for which it is famous the world over. Burton's hops come mainly from Herefordshire, and its barley from Norfolk.

Until recently there were some twenty breweries in the town, although the present tendency towards amalgamation has reduced this number. The most important breweries were those of the well known firms of Bass and Worthington, each of which had its own railway system. The many level crossings in the town were in frequent use to allow the passage of a train, headed by an 0-4-0ST, conveying the valuable cargo. The Bass engines were painted a pleasing shade of yellow-brown. This alas is a sight no longer to be seen, as most of the brewery railway systems in Burton have been closed down in favour of road transport, and what little remains is worked by the inevitable diesels.

An old view of a group of Bass shunters at the loco shed, Burton-on-Trent, probably about sixty years ago.

Part of the brewery of Messrs Worthington & Company showing loco No 4.

94

Bass No 11 at the interchange sidings with the MR.

Marston Thompson & Evershed No 3 in 1933.

A Midland 0-4-0ST No 1142A on a beer train
in the streets of Burton-on-Trent before 1907.

95

CROSS COUNTRY AND BRANCH LINES

Having dealt with the principal main lines and chief railway centres of the area comprised by the Midlands, some attention should now be turned to the innumerable byways and branches. So many of these have succumbed during the last decade and their sad remains can nowadays only be identified by former track beds, cuttings and embankments, abandoned and derelict stations, relics of an earlier age of the heyday of railways before the coming of the omnibus and private car.

The Midland had a number of branch lines in the Derby and Nottingham areas, and some of these were amongst the first in the whole country to be ousted by rival bus services, which multiplied in alarming numbers after the first world war. It was sad to see the once well filled, comfortable trains gradually lose their passengers to such an extent that even by the late 1920s most of them were running almost empty, and the gradual withdrawal of passenger services was inevitable. The Ripley branch, which ran parallel with the main road from Derby, was an early example. As soon as the buses appeared, the passengers deserted the railway, probably because of the more frequent omnibus services and the fact that Derby station was less convenient for the shopping centre of the town than was the bus terminal. Consequently Ripley lost its passenger service in 1930, one of the very first casualties of its kind, to be followed in later years by the mass withdrawals which have now bereft the country of all but a handful of true branch services, although many of them survived through the war years. Another instance in the same area was the little township of Heanor, formerly served by both the Midland and Great Northern Railways. The MR passenger service went as long ago as 1926, trams rather than buses forming the competition in this case. When the GNR branch also lost its passenger service in December 1939, Heanor, with a population approaching 15,000, gained the unenviable distinction of being about the largest town in the country without a rail service, although it is true that it was still within easy reach of Langley Mill on the Midland's Erewash Valley line. Such examples could be repeated *en masse*; these two are given as pinpointing the early trend of what was to come.

In more recent times the fate of cross country lines running through sparsely populated areas has been much the same. Here again, both passenger and freight facilities have disappeared and the lines either abandoned altogether or stumps retained to give access to some industrial concern or other. A representative selection of views in the following pages gives examples of these byeways.

Harby and Stathern, a typical wayside station on the old GNR and LNWR joint line, over which passenger services ceased in 1953.

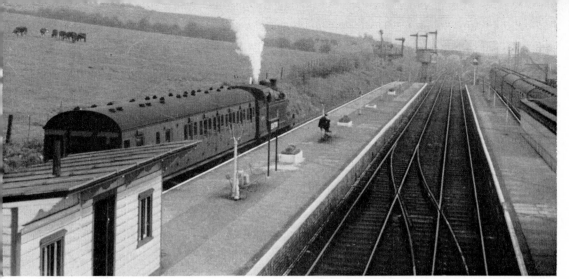

A pleasant and peaceful scene such as has now entirely disappeared. Seaton Junction, on the LNWR Rugby-Peterborough line, where the branch train for Uppingham quietly simmers in the bay platform, awaiting the connecting main line service. This view, taken in 1959, shows the train in the hands of a LT&SR type 4-4-2T No 41975.

Ilkeston Town, one of the many Midland branches which have lost their passenger service. A view taken in 1932; even then the thin complement of passengers seems to consist mainly of local workmen who are obviously too interested in the day's racing results to pay any attention to the photographer, a comparatively rare sight on the railway scene in those days. This branch service survived until 1947.

Another small branch in the district was the Great Northern one from Ilkeston to Heanor. This view was taken in December 1926; the engine is Stirling 0-6-0 No 4032.

A reminder of former days at Melton Mowbray, also on the GNR and LNWR joint railway. The inscription on the door reads 'Refreshment Room, 2nd Class' and is a relic of the days when it was customary to provide separate refreshment rooms for different class passengers, 1st and 3rd, and also, as in this case, where the genuine 2nd class still lingered. The photograph was taken in 1953, but even by that date the refreshment rooms had long since been closed. Such facilities are nowadays only provided at the principal main line stations.

Saxby Junction in 1959, showing the point of divergence of the MR main line to London, via Melton Mowbray, and the branch to Bourne and Spalding. This line although MR property as far as Little Bytham, was for practical purposes the western extremity of the Midland & Great Northern joint railway, that long straggling line through the rural countryside of the eastern counties, which eventually finished up at Lowestoft, some 143 miles from its western extremity.

Another interesting cross-country route in the Midlands was the ambitious Lancashire, Derbyshire & East Coast Railway. This never achieved either of its geographical ambitions for it extended no further than Chesterfield in the west and Lincoln in the east, and was absorbed by the Great Central in 1907. It lost its passenger services in the 1950s, and most of the line is now abandoned. This view shows a train from Lincoln at Dukeries Junction in 1946, headed by GNR 4-4-2T No 4531.

The old Hull & Barnsley Railway was another line which did not live up to its title, in that it did not quite reach Barnsley, the connection being made at Cudworth on the Midland main line. Its passenger services ran only over the main line between Hull and Cudworth (with certain through services to Sheffield) and a branch to Wath. The latter ceased in 1929 and this view shows Wath station as it was in 1947.

A scene on the lovely LNWR branch from Buxton to Ashbourne (now closed) in 1953. The engine is Fowler 2-6-4T No 42368.

The fine steel trestle viaduct at Hunnington on the Halesowen branch near Birmingham, jointly operated by the MR and the GWR. The photograph, taken in 1939, shows a workmen's train with pannier tank No 2718.

The Midland operated the freight traffic, and this view, taken in 1939, shows Kirtley goods No 22579. The line is now closed and the viaduct demolished.

An outpost of the GWR was its cross-country line from Wellington to Nantwich, from which point it ran its trains over the LNWR into Crewe. Here is 2-4-0 No 3223, leaving Market Drayton in 1933.

Another interesting GWR cross-country line was that from Shrewsbury to Worcester; the section between Buildwas and Bewdley was usually known as the Severn Valley line. It lost its passenger and freight service in 1963 and seemed destined to follow the fate of so many similar, secondary lines. Fortunately the Severn Valley Railway Society came into being in 1965, with the ultimate result that part of the route between Bridgnorth and Hampton Loade would re-open under these private auspices. Negotiations for a Light Railway Order are in progress as these lines are being written. Now incorporated as the Severn Valley Railway Co Ltd, it already owns several interesting engines. Of the half dozen or so standard-gauge branches in the country now being operated by private societies this is the only one situated in the Midlands (and that only marginally so). Mention should also be made of the Foxhill Light Railway Society which operates a private line nearly four miles long at Dilham, near Stoke-on-Trent, with a locomotive in steam about two Sundays in the month during the summer season. Also the Railway Preservation Society, of Chasewater, Staffs, mainly concerned with the preservation of interesting locomotives, but with an occasional 'open day' in the summer with engines in steam.

This view shows a train near Bridgnorth in 1962, when normal services were still operating, hauled by standard 2-6-4T No 80079.

Apart from the Manifold Valley Light Railway, already dealt with in chapter 19, the only other steam operated, narrow-gauge, passenger-carrying line in the Midlands was the Ashover Light Railway. It was a latecomer on the scene, being opened as late as 7 April 1925; in fact, one of the last new railways, standard or narrow-gauge, to be built in this country. The 7½ mile line was made to connect Ashover, a small and pleasant country town near Chesterfield, with the MR main line at Clay Cross. Unfortunately it came too late; road transport was already well established by this time, and after a comparatively short life, passenger trains ceased in September 1936 and the line closed altogether in 1950. The six locomotives, which were obtained second hand, had been built in the USA in 1917 for use during the first World War. The gauge was 2 ft. The illustration shows **Joan,** one of these 4-6-0Ts, and a coach, at Ashover in 1926.

The Dearne Valley railway, a twenty-mile long branch from Wakefield to Edlington, near Doncaster, was a busy line through a rich coalfield in South Yorkshire. As well as heavy coal traffic, it also had a passenger service until 1951, and this view, taken in 1932, shows a train formed of a Lancashire & Yorkshire steam railcar, at one of the halts.

Although operated by conventional electric tramcars, the Burton & Ashby was in fact a light railway and was owned by the Midland. It ran mostly on reserved track through the countryside, rather than along public roads in the manner of an urban tramway. This view was taken in 1915. The line had been opened on 2 July 1906, and was closed on 19 February 1927.

Ashby-de-la-Zouch, the Midland Railway station in 1957, when the tram tracks of the Burton & Ashby Light Railway had not yet been removed from the forecourt.

Although they cannot be classified as railways in the general sense, no account would be complete without reference to the numerous steam operated trams which abounded in the Black Country until around the close of the century. Most were later electrified, eventually in their turn to be abandoned in favour of road omnibuses. The picture shows a typical scene in Birmingham about seventy years ago.

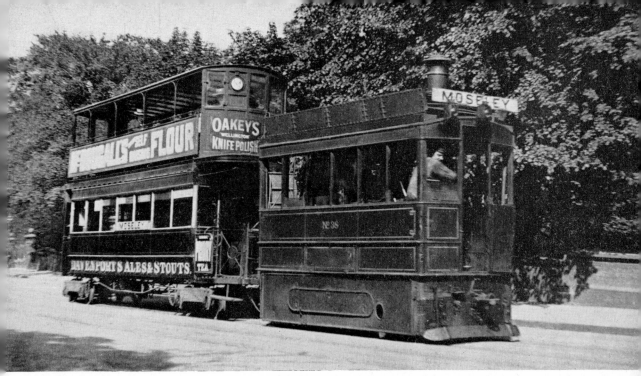

A Birmingham Central Tramways' (later City of Birmingham Tramways Co) tram on the Moseley route, probably about 1900. The engine is No 38, built by Falcon in 1885.

Inclined passenger lifts, which just come within the category of railways, are almost invariably to be found on cliffs at seaside resorts; probably Britain's only inland one is at Bridgnorth. This is an early view and the car seems on this occasion to be conveying goods, but nowadays the passenger accommodation is modernised and completely enclosed.

THE MODERN IMAGE

The railway scene in this country has completely changed during the last twenty years. First there was the gradual introduction of diesel railcars to replace the local steam-hauled train which had been a familiar and endearing sight for as long as anyone now alive can remember. Then, in 1956, came the decision to eliminate steam working altogether from the nationalised railway system; an objective which was reached in 1968, well ahead of the original schedule. To complete the story, a few typical, modern views depict the rail scene as it is today.

English Electric type 4 diesel No 304, with an up express about to enter Beechwood Tunnel on the Birmingham-Coventry line, 1961.

'Peak' class diesel No D27 on the up 'Cornishman' on the Lickey Incline, 1964.

Experimental Sulzer diesel No D 0260, **Lion,** built by the Birmingham Railway Carriage & Waggon Co at Solihull in 1962.

Single-unit diesel railcar No W 55005 on the Severn Valley line, near Eardington, 1963.

An up express leaving Birmingham New Street, with electric locomotive No E3075.

ACKNOWLEDGMENTS

Reproduction of paintings by C. Hamilton-Ellis by courtesy of BR Publicity, Euston: 11 (top), 13 (bottom), 19 (centre), 22 (top, centre and bottom), 27 (centre), 29 (top), 44 (top)

Other illustrations by courtesy of BR Publicity, Euston: 11 (bottom left and right), 13 (top), 14 (top and bottom), 15 (centre and bottom), 16 (bottom), 18 (bottom), 20 (top and bottom), 25 (top), 22 (centre), 44 (centre), 49 (top and bottom), 62 (top), 66, 69 (top), 73 (centre and bottom), 83 (bottom), 84 (top), 108 (bottom)

W. Leslie Good	8, 29 (bottom), 40 (centre), 64 (top)
LGRP	12 (top), 19 (bottom), 45 (bottom), 52 (top), 73 (top), 81 (bottom), 86 (top)
H. C. Casserley	15 (top), 27 (top), 33 (centre and bottom), 34 (top), 36 (centre), 37 (top), 40 (bottom), 41 (centre), 42 (top and bottom), 44 (bottom), 45 (top), 46 (top and bottom), 54 (top and centre), 55 (top, centre and bottom), 57 (bottom), 58 (top), 59 (top, centre and bottom), 62 (bottom), 64 (centre), 65 (top and bottom), 67 (bottom), 71 (top and bottom), 74 (top right and centre), 75 (top and bottom), 77 (top, centre and bottom), 80 (centre and bottom), 81 (top and centre), 86 (bottom), 87 (top left and right, centre and bottom), 88 (bottom), 90 (top, centre and bottom), 91 (top, centre and bottom), 92 (bottom), 93 (top and centre), 95 (top and centre), 96 (bottom), 97 (top, centre and bottom), 98 (top and bottom), 99 (top), 100 (top and bottom), 101 (top and bottom), 103 (top and bottom), 104 (centre)
Walsall Library	16 (top)
Locomotive Publishing Co	24 (bottom), 28 (bottom), 32 (top), 53 (bottom), 80 (top)
W. Shaw, Burslem	28 (top)
Allcock Collection	31 (top)
J. G. Adam	31 (bottom)
H. J. Salmon	32 (bottom)
R. M. Casserley	36 (bottom), 37 (centre), 67 (centre), 75 (centre), 93 (bottom)
Leicester Museum, 'The Newton Collection'	38, 39 (top and bottom)
E. Pouteau	41 (bottom)
M. Mensing	47, 48 (top and bottom), 50 (top and bottom), 51 (top and bottom), 69 (bottom), 84 (bottom), 102, 106, 107 (top and bottom), 108 (top)
News Chronicle	58 (bottom)
Naden, Chesterfield	61
W. A. Camwell	64 (bottom), 99 (bottom)
M. W. Earley	70 (top and bottom)
George Dow	82 (from *The Great Central Railway*, vol. 1), 83 (top)
J. T. Foxall	105 (bottom)

The picture used for the jacket and frontispiece
was painted by Victor Welch

INDEX